BEHIND THE SCENES
SPECIAL EFFECTS

Jillian Powell

Editorial Consultant – Cliff Moon

RISING★STARS

nasen
NASEN House, 4/5 Amber Business Village, Amber Close,
Amington, Tamworth, Staffordshire B77 4RP

Rising Stars UK Ltd.
22 Grafton Street, London W1S 4EX
www.risingstars-uk.com

Every effort has been made to trace copyright holders and
obtain their permission for use of copyright material. The
publisher will gladly receive information enabling them to
rectify any error or omission in subsequent editions.
All facts are correct at time of going to press.

First published 2006
Reprinted 2007

Cover design: Button plc
Cover image: 20th Century Fox / The Kobal Collection
Illustrator: Bill Greenhead
Text design and typesetting: Marmalade Book Design
(www.marmaladebookdesign.com)
Educational consultants: Cliff Moon, Lorraine Petersen and
Paul Blum
Technical consultant: Susan Ellacot and Saul Mahoney
Pictures: AKG Images: pages 6, 25, 27, 31
Alamy: page 35
The Kobal Collection: pages 4, 6, 7, 8, 9, 10, 11, 12, 16, 17,
18, 19, 21, 24, 25, 26, 27, 28, 30, 34, 35, 40, 41, 42, 43, 46
Nimba Creations: page 14

British Library Cataloguing in Publication Data.
A CIP record for this book is available from the British
Library.

ISBN: 978-1-84680-047-1

Printed by Craftprint International Ltd., Singapore

Contents

SFX: art and science

Dinosaurs crash through the jungle.

Aliens land on Earth.

Humans fly and buildings explode.

Films make the impossible look real.

They do it with special effects — or SFX for short.

Film-makers have always used special effects.

1

The camera stopped filming as the axe fell on Mary's head.

2

The actors froze.

3

A dummy was put in Mary's place.

4

Then the camera started up as the head fell.

Specs and smells

The 1950s

In the 1950s, the cinema was full of special effects!

People wore special glasses to watch 3D films.

Cinema seats gave small electric shocks.

Smell-o-Vision pipes pumped smells into cinemas.

The 1970s

Earthquake (1975) shook people in their seats by using loud sounds.

Blockbuster movies such as **Star Wars**, **Superman** and **Close Encounters of the Third Kind** had amazing SFX!

The 1990s

The big screen got bigger with IMAX!

How do they do it?

1 A special camera shoots film that is ten times bigger than usual.

2 The film is shown on a giant screen.

Stop-motion

Stop-motion is one of the oldest SFX.
It is still used today.

Corpse Bride (2005)

How do they do it?

1. A camera shoots in single **frames**.

2. The model is moved a bit between each **frame**.

3. The **frames** are run at movie speed —
   the object looks as if it's moving.

Stop-motion greats:

King Kong (1933)

Chicken Run (2000) →

Corpse Bride (2005)

Ray Harryhausen

Ray Harryhausen was the first film-maker to use stop-motion in **live-action** movies.

His films show actors with dinosaurs, flying saucers and fighting skeletons.

Jason and the Argonauts (1963)

Harryhausen greats:

It Came from Beneath the Sea (1955)

Jason and the Argonauts (1963)

Clash of the Titans (1981)

Harryhausen tributes

Harryhausen's name is on a model piano in **Corpse Bride** (2005) and **Wallace & Gromit in The Curse of the Were-Rabbit** (2005).

In **Monsters, Inc.** (2001) Mike takes his girlfriend to 'Harry Hausen's' restaurant!

King Kong

Stop-motion was used in **King Kong** (1933).

The film tells the story of a giant ape who is captured in the jungle and taken to New York. Then he escapes.

How did they do it?

1. They filmed models of King Kong in tiny **sets** of the jungle and New York.

2. They projected these scenes onto a big screen.

3. They filmed actors on full-size **sets** in front.

Rear projection

Projector — Actor — Screen — Camera

4. Sometimes, they filmed actors on **set** first.

5. They projected these scenes onto a screen. Models and **props** were filmed in front.

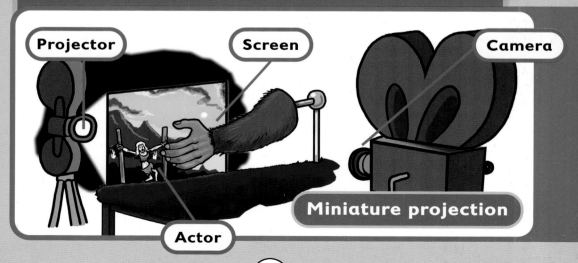

Projector — Screen — Camera

Miniature projection

Actor

Animatronics

Animatronics are puppets or models that move.

How do they do it?

1. Some animatronics have moving parts inside.

2. The animatronic may have a steel frame, such as the T-Rex here.

3. A puppeteer uses a computer to make the parts move.

SFX fact!

Some animatronics have an actor inside who makes the parts move.

Animatronics were used for some of the dinosaurs in **Jurassic Park III** (2001).

They had plastic and steel frames covered in foam rubber skin.

Stunt artists

Stunt artists stand in for actors when the action heats up.

The Mummy Returns (2001)

Famous stunts

The bus jumps a gap in the freeway, **Speed** (1994).

James Bond bungee jumps from the Hoover Dam, **GoldenEye** (1995).

Indiana Jones jumps from his horse on to a moving tank, **Indiana Jones and the Last Crusade** (1989).

Stunt artists need these things to keep them safe.

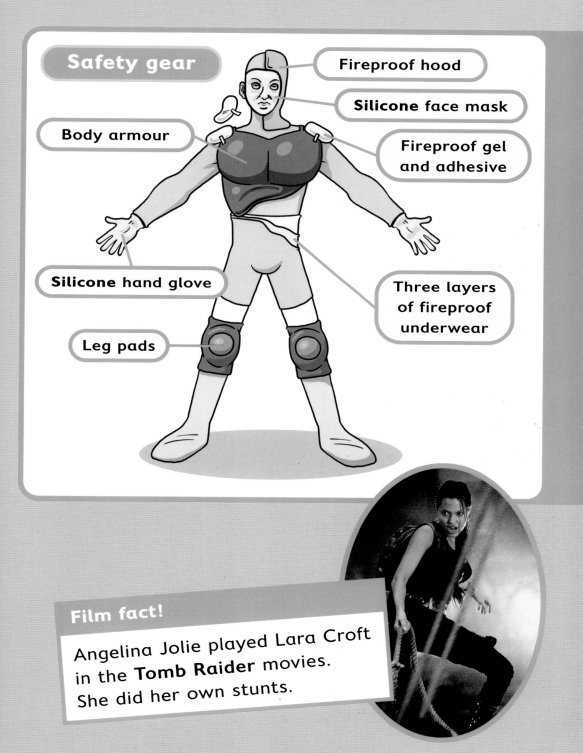

Safety gear

Fireproof hood

Silicone face mask

Body armour

Fireproof gel and adhesive

Silicone hand glove

Three layers of fireproof underwear

Leg pads

Film fact!

Angelina Jolie played Lara Croft in the **Tomb Raider** movies. She did her own stunts.

Machines and props

Films show fires, explosions, floods and hurricanes.

The Day After Tomorrow (2004)

Film-makers use machines and **props** to make these things look real.

Breaking glass

Fire

Special effect	How do they do it?
Hurricane winds	Huge fans – some fans have aircraft engines!
Rain, floods, tidal waves	Pumps and hoses
Fire and smoke	Smoke and flame machines
Dust from explosions	**Mortars** with cement dust inside
Gunshot wounds	Small **charges** that explode with fake blood
Crashing through windows	Fake glass
Snow	Plastic chips, chopped feathers, plaster, paper, cornflakes

Snow

Exploding **mortars**

Blue-screen

In the film **E.T. the Extra-Terrestrial** (1982), a child rides a bicycle through the air.

How did they do it?

The film-maker used blue-screen.

1. The moon was filmed.

2. The child was filmed on the bike against a blue background.

3. A computer cut away the blue background. This left a **matte**.

4. The **matte** was set against the moon background.

Famous blue-screen images

Luke flies the X-wing fighter down the trench of the Death Star, **Star Wars** (1977).

The X-Men finish a practice battle, **X-Men: The Last Stand** (2006).

Riding the Eagle
(Part one)

"So what do we have to do for this project?"
Ravi asked Dan.

"It's a blue-screen shot," Dan said. "I've got a brilliant idea for it. You are riding this massive eagle. It's like a horse. You're in a storm with thunder and lightning and …"

"Me? Why do *I* have to ride the eagle?"
Ravi asked.

"Because *I* am directing!" Dan told him.
"Anyway, you won't really be on an eagle,
you dork. We can't make a massive model of
an eagle. That's the point. We get a shot of an
eagle and a shot of a stormy sky. Then we put
them together."

"And how do we get a shot of an eagle?"
Ravi asked.

Dan tapped his nose. "Don't worry, mate.
I've got it sorted!" he said.

Continued on page 32

CGI

CGI stands for Computer Generated Imagery. CGI uses computers to model characters, objects and backgrounds.

Sky Captain and the World of Tomorrow (2004) had CG backgrounds and live actors. Some of the **props** were CG too!

All the acting was carried out on a blue-screen **set**. The backgrounds were added in afterwards.

The first CG character was a knight in **The Young Sherlock Holmes** (1985).

Toy Story (1995) was the first full-length CG **feature** film.

CG stars:

The water creature from **The Abyss** (1989).

Jar Jar Binks, **Star Wars: Episodes I–III** (1999–2005).

Optimus Prime from **Transformers** (2007)

CGI is used to replace actors in dangerous scenes. It is also used when make-up effects won't work.

Spider-Man 3 (2007)

CGI is also used to make **extras** for big crowd scenes.

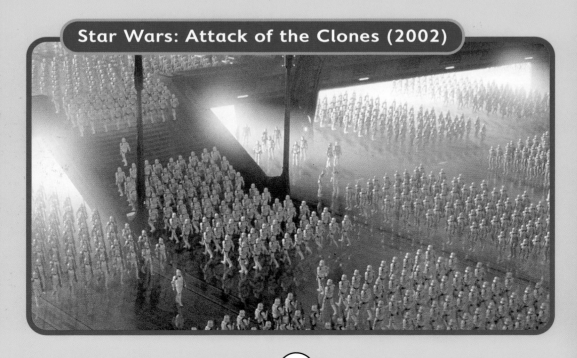
Star Wars: Attack of the Clones (2002)

How do they do it?

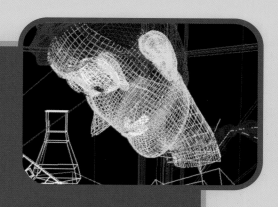

1 3D software makes 'wire frame' models.

2 Colour, texture and lighting are added later.

Famous CG images:

The animal stampede, **Jumanji** (1995).

Passenger **extras** falling from the sinking ship, **Titanic** (1997).

The army of Orcs in **The Lord of the Rings: The Return of the King** (2003).

Johnny Storm takes on the Silver Surfer in **Fantastic Four: Rise of the Silver Surfer** (2007).

Kong reborn

A remake of **King Kong** came out in 2005. It used a lot of CGI and also some models.

The model for Kong had a foam rubber body over a jointed metal frame.

The new Kong had a smaller head and longer legs than the old Kong.

Kong's movements were copied from apes in the wild.

Motion capture

Motion capture helps to give lifelike movements to CG characters.

Gollum from the Lord of the Rings films was 'acted' by Andy Serkis.

How do they do it?

Motion capture turns actors' movements into computer **data**.

1. The actor wears **sensors** at key body joints.

2. Digital cameras track and record the movements of the **sensors**.

3. They send this motion **data** to a computer.

4. The motion **data** is used to make the CG character move like a real person.

Body suit

Sensors

Cybergloves – **sensors** at joints

Riding the Eagle

(Part two)

The next day, Dan took Ravi out. Dan took a camera, too.

"What is this place? Looks a bit like a zoo," Ravi said.

"It's the Bird of Prey Centre," Dan told him. "They have falcons, eagles … the lot. You can watch them fly."

Ravi looked in the cages. Huge birds stared back at them from behind the bars.

"They're evil!" Ravi said. "I don't like the way that one is looking at me!"

"The show is about to start," Dan told him. "They will be flying the birds and feeding them. We have to get a shot of the eagle flying. Easy-peasy."

Three hours later, they were still trying.

Continued on page 36

Morphing

Morphing is when one image changes into another image.

Characters and backgrounds can be morphed.

Pirates of the Caribbean: The Curse of the Black Pearl (2003)

How do they do it?

1. They film actors and models in the same position.

2. The images are laser scanned.

3. The images are marked up at key points — like eyes, nose and mouth.

4. A computer morphs one image into the other by matching the key points.

Famous morphs:

T: 1000 morphing in **Terminator 2: Judgment Day** (1991).

Neo and the mirror in **The Matrix** (1999). ➡

Mystique changes into different characters in the **X-Men** movies (2000–2006).

Film fact!

The first morphing sequence in a film was in **Willow** (1988). It showed Fin Raziel morphing into lots of animals.

Riding the Eagle

(Part three)

Back in town, Dan went through the shots with Ravi.

"The stupid bird! These are no good!" Dan said. "Never mind, I've got a better idea."

He dragged Ravi into a museum.

A bit later, the boys came out again.

"Well, we've got one shot in the bag!" Dan said. He sounded pleased.

"Great! A stuffed eagle!" Ravi said.

"A stuffed eagle that looks like it's flying!" Dan said. "Now we just have to get a shot of you riding something."

"Something?" Ravi asked. He looked worried. "What exactly will I be riding?"

"Don't worry about it," Dan said. "I've got a great idea for that, too. Then we cut out the shots of you and the eagle and put them against that stormy sky. It will be knockout!"

Continued on the next page

"I have never felt so stupid in my life,"
Ravi said.

"Look scared!" Dan told him. "Thunder is
cracking. Lightning is flashing around you
and you're riding a …"

"A *rocking horse*," Ravi cut in. "I'm riding
my kid sister's rocking horse – I feel like
a dipstick!"

"Don't worry about the horse!" Dan said.
"We'll ditch the horse."

Soon it was time for the class to see their film.

Everyone was dead impressed.

"Excellent!" Mrs Baker said. "But this shot is even better. It has a fantasy feel to it …"

Ravi gasped. His mates began to laugh.

"You said you'd ditch the rocking horse!" Ravi hissed at Dan.

"Sorry, mate!" grinned Dan. "Couldn't resist it."

The Matrix trilogy

The Matrix trilogy is a SFX **classic**.

It used a new special effect called 'bullet-time'.

'Bullet-time' shows a scene in 360 degrees and in slow motion.

Film fact!

It took three days to set up Trinity's mid-air kick. They used 120 cameras.

How do they do it?

1 Cameras are set up all around a subject.

2 All the cameras shoot stills.

3 The stills are run as a slow-motion movie.

4 Slowed-down sounds are used with bullet-time shots.

The Matrix (1999)

This scene uses 'bullet-time'.

The Matrix Reloaded (2003)

First use of 3D recording.

The Matrix Revolutions (2003)

Blue-screen and CGI helped to create the huge worlds in the final film.

What next for SFX?

SFX are changing all the time. Take a look at the SFX of the future!

Gollums galore

Fantastic Four: Rise of the Silver Surfer (2007)

'Vactors' are virtual actors.

They will replace real actors in many movies.

Film fact!

Hair, fabrics and human emotions are the hardest effects to capture in CGI.

Virtual worlds

Moviemakers will develop new ways to create virtual worlds.

Even the world as we know it will start to look different.

X-Men: The Last Stand (2006)

3D IMAX

Filmgoers will wear special goggles to watch 3D IMAX.

You will see huge dinosaurs 'eating' off your lap!

Quiz

1 What is a matte?

2 Name three things that can be used to look like snow.

3 What does CGI stand for?

4 What was the first fully CGI film?

5 Why is blue used in blue-screen?

6 What are animatronics?

7 What is a vactor?

8 What is bullet-time?

9 What is motion capture used for?

10 What does morphing mean?

Glossary of terms

ball-joint   Joint that allows movement in many directions.

charges   Devices that explode.

classic   Does not date – a classic film will always be popular.

data   Information that a computer uses.

extras   People shown in the background of movie scenes.

feature   A full-length film made for cinemas – forty minutes or longer.

frame   Single image on a film reel.

hinges   Joints that allow backward and forward movement.

live action   Movies with live actors in them.

matte   Cut-out of an actor or model used in blue-screen.

mortars   Shells that explode.

props   Things that are used on stage or film sets – like chairs or plates.

sensors   Devices that send or receive signals.

sets   The background scenes built for movies.

silicone   A strong, skin-like material that can stretch.

More resources

Books

Special Effects: An Introduction to Movie Magic
Ron Miller
Published by Lerner Publishing Company (ISBN: 0761329188)

Yikes! Scariest Stunts Ever
Jesse Leon McCann
Published by Scholastic (ISBN: 0439803489)

A look at some of the most spectacular stunts ever performed.

The Art of 'The Matrix'
Larry Wachowski, et al
Published by Titan Books (ISBN: 1840231734)

Drawings, storyboards and cut scenes from The Matrix trilogy.

Magazines

Empire, EMAP
The UK's best-selling movie magazine, features all the upcoming releases with on-set reports.

Websites

www.hotwired.com/webmonkey/kids/lessons/animation.html
Online lessons in animation techniques.

www.cgchannel.com
Interviews with visual effects artists and loads of film news.

www.ilm.com
The official website for SFX company Industrial Light and Magic.

DVDs and Videos

The Matrix Revisited (2001)
Warner Home Video (Cat. No. B00005U0HV)

Two hours of behind-the-scenes footage from the original **Matrix** film.

Answers

1 A cut-out of an actor or model used in blue-screen.

2 Any three from plastic chips, chopped feathers, plaster, paper, cornflakes.

3 Computer Generated Imagery.

4 Toy Story.

5 It contrasts with the colour of skin.

6 Models or puppets that can be worked by a computer or actor.

7 A virtual actor.

8 A way of showing a scene in 360 degrees in slow motion.

9 To give lifelike movements to CG characters.

10 Changing one image into another on screen.

Index